RECOVERING FROM DIVORCE

RECOVERING FROM DIVORCE

DAVID A. THOMPSON

BETHANY HOUSE PUBLISHERS
MINNEAPOLIS, MINNESOTA 55438
A Division of Bethany Fellowship, Inc.

Recovering from Divorce

David A. Thompson

ISBN 0-87123-476-9

Published by Bethany House Publishers
A Division of Bethany Fellowship, Inc.
6820 Auto Club Road, Minneapolis, Minn. 55438

Printed in the United States of America

Dedication

I dedicate this book to the many men and women of the United States Navy who have shared with me their pain and grief over becoming "suddenly single." Their courage, faith and commitment to move the mountains of anger, self-pity and doubt from their lives have been the inspiration for this book. Their strategies for "getting on with life" have provided much of the material which will help others recover from divorce. To these brave souls I am deeply indebted.

About the Author

David A. Thompson is a chaplain serving in the United States Navy. He has been a parish pastor, hospital chaplain, Bible school teacher, and assistant editor for a religious book publisher.

He received a B.S. from the University of Wisconsin (Superior) in 1968; attended Trinity Evangelical Divinity School and the Lutheran Brethren Seminary, graduating from the latter with a M.Div. degree in 1971; received a M.S.E. degree in Counseling from the University of Wisconsin (Oshkosh) in 1976; and presently is a D.Min. candidate at Trinity Evangelical Divinity School. He is an ordained minister of the Free Methodist Church of North America.

He is married and the father of three boys.

The author has written a counseling guide for couples contemplating marriage entitled *A Premarital Guide for Couples and Their Counselors* (Bethany House Publishers, 1979), and a counseling guide for married couples entitled *Five Steps Toward a Better Marriage* (Bethany House Publishers, 1980).

Foreword

As a counselor, pastor and chaplain, David Thompson has spent many hours with men and women who are going through the pain of divorce. He has seen their discouragements, struggles and feelings of failure—and he has been able to help them move toward hope and recovery. This book does not defend or condone divorce, or take a light view of marriage. The author has a high view of marriage coupled with a deep sensitivity for those whose marriages have failed. With compassion, insight, and creativity, he has produced a workbook which—when used alone, in a group, or with a counselor—can gently lead divorced and divorcing people toward divine forgiveness, personal growth and new beginnings.

Dr. Gary Collins
Chairman, Dept. of Pastoral Counseling & Psychology
Trinity Evangelical Divinity School

Table of Contents

Introduction

Divorce is one of the most painful words in the English language. It denotes a rending, a tearing of relationships. It results in heart-wrenching grief and anger for all involved. Few of us remain untouched by this painful phenomenon sweeping through our society.

We Christians are caught in a unique tension regarding divorce. On one hand, the Church calls us to be prophetic, supporting and defending the biblical institution of marriage. We find ourselves reluctant to lower our standards, to accommodate ourselves to a covenant-breaking, "throw-away" society. We strongly sense the need to be "salt," preserving society from decay. We feel the need to proclaim God's standard of righteousness in a world suffering from a bad case of "moral amnesia." On the other hand, we are called to a pastoral care that feels the pain of suffering; that understands the grief caused by sin against another; that knows the grace that liberates; and that reaches out in unconditional acceptance and binds the wounds of the broken. Here we find ourselves called to be light, charged with showing people the way back to the Father's house and heart. How then do we resolve this tension that binds us in inaction and passivity, amidst a world full of pain and grief?

In a world where one out of three marriages ends in divorce, it seems strange that the Church tends to exclude this large portion of society from the grace of God. Divorce has been relegated to the status of an "unpardonable sin." Persons who have been divorced are often subjected to a hostility and rejection which is unbecoming in those who call themselves Christians. This is particularly disturbing when there is little biblical evidence to support the "unpardonable" implications with which this sin is surrounded.

I am not attempting to defend divorce! I believe it represents a moral failure for both parties involved. Yet the fact remains, right or wrong, divorces are taking place daily, often among people respected for their Christian testimony. My perspective is pastoral rather than judicial. It is aimed at bringing healing and spiritual wholeness to the bruised and broken. I do admit that the "accident" of divorce happens, due to negligence, malice, or treacherous environmental conditions. My role is not so much to assess degrees of blame as it is to bandage the wounds and help people recover from a very painful experience. Hopefully in the process we can assess what went wrong with an eye to forgiveness and repentance for past action.

This book is designed to be used by pastors and counselors to care for the divorced in a sensitive and loving manner. The author cannot take responsibility for how this manual is used. It is his hope that the intent of the pastor-counselor be that of helping rather than hurting. One should seek additional assistance from the helping professions when necessary to effect healing in broken lives.

How To Use This Book

Philosophical Issues

This workbook is primarily designed for the use of pastors and counselors in their ministry to divorced people. It is designed to elicit a commitment from the counselee to work on his problems. The thrust of this workbook is decidedly Christian. Its objective is to heal and not to judge. That is not to say a person will not be confronted with destructive and hurtful behavior and encouraged to deal with that behavior. The end product should be forgiveness and restoration, not condemnation and alienation. This book is aimed at a person *recovering* from divorce. It is not intended to be used by a couple contemplating divorce (see author's workbook *Five Steps Toward a Better Marriage* for marriage counseling materials). Also, it is not to be used by a pastor/counselor as a weapon to strike back at someone who has blatantly violated church doctrine on divorce.

I do not believe there is such a thing as "value-free" pastoral counseling. Pastors are called to lead and encourage their congregations to follow Christian ethics. When the "faithful" fail to live up to these principles, the pastor should seek to exhort and guide his flock in ways that honor God. Pastors have the great difficulty of providing care and help for divorced persons consistent with their "prophetic" and "pastoral" office. I believe, with the proper guidelines, that this workbook can address that tension and effectively meet the needs of people who are hurting as a result of divorce.

Guidelines for Individual Counseling

Each section is designed to be completed prior to each interview. Worksheets can be given out by the counselor as whole sections or partial sections, one at a time. Or the counselor can remove the instructional pages which apply to him/her and give the remainder of the book to the counselee to be worked on at his/her own pace. It is important that the completed worksheets be given or mailed to the pastor/counselor *in advance* to allow for evaluation. Such action commits the counselee to the counseling process. It also assists the counselor in narrowing the discussion to those areas that need amplification and further dialogue. This should save the counselor considerable time as well as sharpen the focus of the discussion. This format is helpful in that it asks some tough questions that a non-confrontive person might find hard to ask in verbal form. Also, it eases into the counseling process gradually, focusing on a social/psychological history of the counselee. This assists in building a relational bridge between counselor and counselee. It also provides a context for later questions focused on present behavior and future plans.

Concern may arise over how to handle answers to tough questions, particularly if the answers run counter to the counselor's belief system and theology. Answers which provide evidence of unrepented sin may be hard to deal with (e.g.: an unforgiving spirit, continuing sexual sin, violent and vindictive behavior, or plans for remarriage on grounds perceived as "other than biblical"). Several suggestions can be made here. First, a distinction needs to be made between "sin" and the "sinner." We may not approve of certain behavior, practically or morally. Yet, we must use great care to accept a person where he/she is, not where we would like him/her to be. Sometimes the failings of another may threaten us and our values, and make us uncomfortable with the one who is seeking our help. Hopefully, we can see past the symptomatic behavior to focus our attention on root relational issues between God and man. It is not wrong to address moral failure. But to insist on "right" actions and attitudes at the wrong time will only erase the symptoms without solving the problem. It will lead to masking, dishonesty, alienation and termination of the counseling relationship. In Jesus' terms, the outside of the cup will be cleansed while the inside remains unclean.

Let the counselee share what is happening in his/her life, both positive and negative. Listen for pain, grief and lack of self-fulfillment. Look for emotional patterns—hostility, depression, insecurity and general withdrawal from life. Be sensitive to philosophical assumptions—"Life is fair/unfair"; "Eat-drink-be merry for tomorrow we die"; "There is no right or wrong—just do your thing." Watch for sudden changes in behavior, such as social isolation, suicidal intention, sexual promiscuity, "workaholic" patterns, drug/alcohol abuse, violent/abusive actions toward former spouse and/or children. In all these issues, look for destructive behavior patterns which are preventing significant healing from taking place. Once you have a "feel" for these issues, look for openings to reveal your observations to the person you are seeking to help.

The counselor should also anticipate the kind of answers that may be given to some questions (i.e., lack of forgiveness, a root of bitterness, sexual impropriety, the possibility of dating/remarriage after divorce). Prior to launching into this program, you must involve yourself in biblical research on these issues and be prepared to provide guidance to those who seek your counsel. Seeking to engage in an idealogical debate is discouraged. Through the use of leading questions found on the worksheets, the pastor can help a counselee reflect on his/her behavior and its effect on his/her relationship with the Lord and with others.

Guidelines for Group Counseling

Offering the opportunity for a "Divorce Recovery Group" can open the door of ministry to many untouched by the gospel. It can provide a format for outreach and healing in the community. This will call for a church to openly accept those who have missed the mark through marital failure. This is more than just an intellectual assent to love. It is a call to actively *work* to create an environment which nurtures, supports and guides those recovering from divorce.

In practical terms, instruct each participant to work on each section prior to the group session. Then use the questions under "Group Leader's Guide" to stimulate discussion within the group. If group members have done their homework, they should have no difficulty relating to the general questions in Appendix 1.

General Guidelines

The responsibility for behavior must rest with the counselee. The client must eventually be led to evaluate his/her behavior in the light of his/her relationship to the Lord and His Word. Until reconciliation takes place on the vertical plane with the Lord, it will be impossible to produce a lasting peace between conflicting parties on the horizontal plane.

Recognize that the person you are counseling is at some stage in the grieving process. In one sense, there has been a "death in the family." What once was, is no longer! The result is a whole range of feelings that we lump under the heading of "grief"—guilt, anger, regret, bargaining and finally, resignation and acceptance. The pastor/counselor's task will be to help the client walk through "the valley of the shadow of death" and help him/her begin a new life on the other side of this painful trek.

Give each person the "emotional space" to work through his/her feelings regarding what has happened. Do not be intimidated by tears or outbursts of anger and/or bitterness. This emotional discharging can have a cleansing effect which will clear the air for further discussion and better understanding. Many divorced people have concealed their feelings for too long, for fear of judgment and retribution. Be sensitive, listen for both tone and content in your conversation. Check to see if body language (facial expression, posture, body gestures) reinforces what he/she is saying. Empathize, encourage, exhort and support where you can. Accent the positive, lovingly confront the negative. Commit yourself to praying, thinking, and working toward the goal of spiritual and emotional healing for the person who seeks your help. Enlist other experienced Christians to bring support, nurture and fellowship to the one struggling with the pain of parting.

Above all, gently lead the hurting toward hope! Without hope, without forgiveness, without new beginnings, the human spirit is crushed. We need to call people to repent of destructive, ungodly behavior. We need to point to the promised forgiveness of God. We need to offer the healing hand of love, and help divorced persons reconstruct their lives from the ashes of defeat. May we respond to the challenge to bring the light of the gospel to those sitting in the darkness we call divorce. May we help many put aside the past and begin living in the present to the glory of God. Only in this way can we declare that truly there is life after divorce!

SECTION I

Who Are You?

> *"O Lord, thou hast searched me and known me! Thou knowest when I sit down and when I rise up; thou discernest my thoughts from afar. Thou searchest out my path and my lying down, and art acquainted with all my ways."* Psalm 139:1-3 (RSV)

Where do you begin when telling the story of your life? Do you keep it light and superficial? Do you just stick to the bare facts? Or do you begin to lower your mask and reveal who you really are?

Recognize the fact that *you are already known*! God knows you intimately. He knows your past, present and future. He knows your sorrows and joys, failures and successes and doubts and dreams. He knows everything about you, both good and bad. In the midst of seeing you as you really are, He does not turn away but comes toward you offering His love and acceptance.

Open yourself up to this process of knowing and being known. This starts by being honest with yourself, with others and with the Lord. Only through this kind of risk can healing begin in your life. Use this section to take a good look at yourself. Then take this new knowledge and work to make things better.

Who Are You?

Part 1 – *Your Home*

Describe your first childhood impressions of your home (safe/dangerous, happy/sad, rich/poor). What were your feelings about home? ______

Describe your early experiences in school. What were your feelings about school and your schoolmates?

Positive experiences: ______

Negative experiences: ______

Describe your early experiences in the church. What were your feelings about church?

Positive feelings: ______

Negative feelings: ______

Describe your relationship with your parents (during your early years and teen years). What were your feelings toward them?

Describe your parents. What were they like?

Mother

Positive characteristics:

Negative characteristics:

Father

Positive characteristics:

Negative characteristics:

In what ways did your parents influence your life?

Mother

Positive influences:

Negative influences:

Father

Positive influences: ____

Negative influences: ____

Write in one sentence an epitaph for each of your parents:

"Here lies Mom. She was ____."

"Here lies Dad. He was ____."

Was there a drug-alcohol problem in your home while you were a child? ____________________

If yes, describe how the problem affected you and your family: ____________________

Were you ever physically or sexually abused as a child? If so, what happened, when did it happen, and what was its effect on your life? ____________________

Did you feel that your parents loved each other? If so, how did they show it? If not, how did they demonstrate their lack of love?

What were your feelings regarding your parents' relationship?

Were your parents divorced? ________ If so, when? ____________________

What was the effect of their divorce upon your life? ____________________

Give a brief history of your life (through age 25):

When and where were you born? ____________________

Parents' occupations: ____________________

Sibling relationships: ____________________

Educational experience: ____________________

Major accomplishments: ____________________

Major disappointments: ____________________

Counselor's comments:

Part 2 — *Yourself*

Describe yourself.

Positive traits: ______

Negative traits: ______

In what way would you like to be remembered? Write your own epitaph:

"Here lies ______. He/she was ______."

What kind of image do you think you project when around others (e.g., happy/sad, competent/incompetent, inferior/superior, strong/weak)? ______

Is this image an honest picture of the "real" you? ______

If not, what is? ______

What do you want others to know about you? ______

What about yourself do you want to keep hidden from others? ______

What have you valued most in life? (List in order of importance, from most important to least.)

1. ______
2. ______
3. ______
4. ______
5. ______

What is of very little value to you? ______

What are the major needs in your life? (List in order of importance, from most important to least.)

1. ______
2. ______
3. ______
4. ______
5. ______

In what ways do you sense you are valuable? (What would people miss by not knowing you or not having you around?) ______

What have you done to help people know you better? ______

What usually makes you angry? (List five things.)

1. ______
2. ______
3. ______
4. ______
5. ______

In what ways do you show your anger (pout/scream, silence/discussion, violence/run away)? ______________________________

What generally happens when you express your anger? ______________________________

What have you done to bring joy to your life? ______________________________

What have been your goals in life? (List in order of importance, from most important to least.)

1. ______________________________
2. ______________________________
3. ______________________________
4. ______________________________
5. ______________________________

Describe the most significant experience in your life: ______________________________

Why was it so meaningful to you? ______________________________

Counselor's Comments:

Part 3 — *Others*

Describe the person who has had the greatest impact on your life. What did he/she do that was so meaningful? ____

What kind of persons did you date prior to meeting your former spouse? (List first names and positive/negative characteristics of two people.)

Name: __________

Positive characteristics: __________

Negative characteristics: __________

Name: __________

Positive characteristics: __________

Negative characteristics: __________

What kind of people have you chosen for friends? (Shared interests, personality traits, etc.) __________

Do you believe in God? ______ If yes, what do you mean by "believe" and how has this belief affected your life? If no, why not? __________

In what ways have you grown spiritually throughout your life? __________

In what areas do you sense need for further growth?

Describe your relationship to God to date:

What are the major issues about which God is dealing with you right now?

What are you doing in your devotional/prayer life during this time? (Portions of scripture you are reading, prayer topics)

What have you been doing for Christian fellowship and witness?

Fellowship:

Witness:

How do you envision God's character? (strong, but mean; loving, but weak; loving and strong; weak and mean)? Select one. Give reasons from personal experience for your selection.

Counselor's Comments:

SECTION II

Where Have You Been?

"The Lord is merciful and gracious, slow to anger and abounding in steadfast love. He will not always chide, nor will He keep His anger forever. He does not deal with us according to our sins, nor requite us according to our iniquities. For as the heavens are high above the earth, so great is His steadfast love toward those who fear Him; as far as the east is from the west, so far does He remove our transgressions from us. As a father pities his children, so the Lord pities those who fear Him. For He knows our frame; He remembers that we are dust."
Psalm 103:8-14 (RSV)

The past! Often it's not what you would have planned for your life, particularly if it has been marked by bad choices, angry voices and many painful experiences. You may live with regrets, wishing a lot of attitudes and actions could be retrieved from the past like so many feathers scattered from a torn pillow.

The past cannot be relived. But you can learn from your failures as you challenge the changeable and accept the unchangeable. You can look to the Lord for strength in this matter. He can give you the courage to look at your past, by assuring you of His unconditional love and understanding. He can help you repent of destructive behavior, seeking forgiveness and offering it in return. By feeling His loving acceptance, you can begin to accept yourself again. Through His forgiveness you can shake off the shackles of guilt which bind you. You can begin to experience a new spiritual freedom which will help you to rebuild your life from the ashes of defeat. Only as you deal with your past before the Lord can you have any expectation of new beginnings. May God give you His grace in the days ahead to forgive and to be forgiven.

Where Have You Been?

Part 1 – *Your Hopes*

How did you meet your former spouse, and what attracted you to him/her?

Describe your courtship:

Length:

Interests shared:

Disagreements:

Ways you dealt with conflict:

Feelings during courtship about readiness to marry:

Sense of personal worth (Did you feel your partner would be privileged to get you for a spouse?):

Appreciation of your fiancé/fiancée (Did you count yourself privileged to be gaining your partner as a spouse?):

Did you trust your fiancé/fiancée?

Did you love your former spouse prior to marriage?

If so, in what ways did you show your love? If not, why did you mask your true feelings?

What made you finally decide to marry your former spouse?

Did you have to get married due to pregnancy? ____________ If so, did you question whether your spouse really loved you for yourself? ____________ How did you respond to this? ____________

What was your former spouse like?

Positive character traits: ____________

Negative character traits: ____________

Before you were married, what did you believe you could contribute to your relationship?

What kind of contribution to your relationship did you expect your spouse to make?

What interests did you/your spouse have that were not shared?

How did this affect your relationship? ____________

When and where were you married? ____________

What expectations were brought to your marriage?

By you: ____________

By your spouse: ____________

What needs did you see in your spouse's life after you were married?

What did you do to meet those needs?

Describe your first year of marriage.

Communication:

Finances:

Social life:

Sexual life:

Spiritual life:

What love expressions from your courtship diminished after you were married?

What did you enjoy about each other?

What goals did you share?

What goals were not shared?

What values did you share? ______________________________

____

____

What values were not shared? ______________________________

____

____

Counselor's Comments:

Part 2 — *Your Sorrows*

Describe your arguments.

What did you disagree about the most? ______

In what ways did you express your disagreement (yell, pout, cry, hit, etc.)? ______

Who usually made the first move toward reconciliation and what did he/she do? ______

Were there any "unpardonable sins" that you held against each other? ______

If so, what were they and why were they unpardonable?

When did you begin to sense trouble in your marriage? ______

What issues contributed to the beginnings of trouble? ______

What were your feelings toward saving your marriage? ______

What attempts were made to save your marriage?

By you: ______

By your former spouse:

In what ways did you contribute to the breakdown in your marriage?

In what ways did your former spouse contribute to the breakdown in your marriage?

In retrospect, what do you believe were the underlying *expectations, beliefs*, and *attitudes* which contributed in a major way to your breakup?

Expectations (what you expected of yourself/your spouse in your marriage):

Beliefs (what you believed your world and your marriage should offer you):

Attitudes (the spirit in which you/your spouse approached your relationship):

When was a decision made to seek a divorce?

What factors were involved in the divorce decision? (How did you, at the time, rationalize that this was a wise decision?)

Who initiated legal action and upon what basis was the suit made?

What were your feelings about yourself and your spouse once divorce papers were filed?

When was the divorce granted and what was the judgment of the court regarding financial responsibility and visitation rights?

Have the legal obligations of the court decree been honored by all concerned? If not, what has not been honored?

Why not?

In what ways has the divorce affected your close relationships?

With your parents/siblings

With your in-laws

With your friends

With your children

What has been the emotional impact of the divorce upon your children? (changes in behavior, ways they express their feelings)

In what ways have you tried to help them through this difficult time?

In what ways has your divorce affected your former spouse's relationship with your children?

What have you done to prevent your children from being turned against your former spouse?

What have you done to thwart you and your spouse playing the role of "Santa Claus" (the parent without custody bringing expensive gifts to win the children's hearts) or "Prison Warden" (the parent with custody who becomes known by the children as a tough disciplinarian)?

What kind of problems emerge for you in encountering your former spouse socially or for business reasons?

____

____

____

____

____

____

Counselor's Comments:

Part 3 – *Your Circumstances*

Describe your financial situation.

In what ways has your divorce affected you economically? ______________________

What have you done about your financial situation? ______________________

In what ways has your divorce affected you spiritually?

____

How have you been treated by the church?

Positively: ______________________

Negatively: ______________________

What are your feelings regarding the church in the aftermath of your divorce? ______________________

In what ways have you dealt with the problems of solo parenting?

Discipline: ______________________

Child care: ______

Recreation/quality time: ______

Male/Female role models: ______

Conflict betweeen employment and parenting: ______

What kind of social life have you had since you have been divorced?

What are your feelings about dating again? ______

Are you dating again? ______ If so, describe the kind of people you are dating.

Positive characteristics: ______

Negative characteristics: ______

In what ways are they similar/dissimilar to your former spouse? ______

What kind of difficulties do you encounter in dating again after being "out of circulation" for some time? ______

What kind of difficulties have you had in revealing your emotions to another person of the opposite gender since your divorce?

Have people tried to take advantage of your emotional vulnerability by trying to exploit you sexually?

In what ways have you dealt with this problem?

In what ways have you dealt with your need for emotional and spiritual fulfillment?

Do you believe you can love and be loved again?

What makes you lovable?

Have you had or do you now have a drug/alcohol problem?

If so, describe:

When did the problem start?

Frequency of use:

Amount of use:

In what ways did this affect your former marriage?

In what ways does it affect your present life-style?

What have you done about your problem?

Counselor's Comments:

SECTION III

What Are You Thinking and Feeling?

"*Create in me a new, clean heart, O God, filled with clean thoughts and right desires. Don't toss me aside, banished forever from your presence. Don't take your Holy Spirit from me. Restore to me again the joy of your salvation, and make me willing to obey you.*" Psalm 51:10-12 (TLB)

Divorce can create a terrible, emotional firestorm in your life. This conflagration can dramatically affect the way you think and feel about yourself and your world. You can quickly be ravaged by blazing anger and hatred, smothered by the fumes of depression, and crushed by the debris of guilt.

It is important to take charge of the way you think and feel. This starts with willingly offering your mind and spirit to the care and control of the Lord. You need to selectively embrace those things that positively build your spirit and reject those things that destroy your peace. This means taking positive steps toward the heart of God, to allow Him to cleanse and renew you, making joy a part of your life again.

This process of renewal begins by looking at the way you look at life. Feelings tend to follow in "piggyback" fashion the way you view your world. What you tell yourself about your world has a dramatic effect on how you feel. You need to examine your beliefs about yourself, others and God. From that perspective, you can begin to see how your perception of your circumstances is often colored positively or negatively.

Work through this section with an eye to seeing what you believe and how that affects you and those around you.

What Are You Thinking and Feeling?

Part 1 — *Your Feelings*

In what ways are you dealing with your anger?

Toward your former spouse ______

Toward yourself ______

Did you and do you still feel rejected following your divorce? ______ If so, how are you dealing with these feelings? ______

Do you feel guilty for actions surrounding your separation? ______

If so, what are you doing to deal with the guilt and the feelings that accompany it? ______

What did you do specifically that makes you feel guilty? ______

Grief (whether by death or divorce) generally has several stages—disbelief/denial, bargaining, anger, despair/depression, acceptance. Describe where you believe you are in the grieving process: ______

Have you had a "funeral" for your past relationship? ______ If so, describe how you finally "laid to rest" your relationship and began to get on with your life. If not, describe evidence which gives you hope for a resurrection and a new life together with your former spouse or separated spouse.

Can you honestly give up your "right" to anger and hatred, and forgive your former spouse for his/her attitudes and actions?

If you can, when will you do it and how will you do it?

If you can't, what prevents you from offering forgiveness?

Have you asked your former spouse for forgiveness for your part in the breakup?

If not, why not?

If so, was forgiveness granted? Have you accepted that forgiveness?

Have you asked God for forgiveness for your part in the breakup? When?

If not, why not?

What do you believe is necessary to do to be forgiven by God?

Do you believe you can be forgiven for your actions and attitudes? Why do you believe this?

Have you forgiven yourself for the pain you caused yourself? If not, why not?

Can you pray for your former spouse and his/her needs? ________________ Do you? ____________

What specific needs are you aware of and what are you praying for regarding those needs? ____________

How do you deal with the depression related to divorce action? ____________

What do you do to handle the judgment of others regarding your divorce? ____________

What person has been the biggest help to you during this time? ____________

What has he/she done, or not done, that has been helpful? ____________

Counselor's Comments:

Part 2 — *Your Thinking*

If there is such a thing as "lessons learned" from divorce, what do you think they would be in your case?

What are you doing to "unpack" mentally and get on with your life?

Memory can be a blessing and a curse. Pause for a moment and list both positive and negative memories of your former marriage relationship.

Positive memories:

Negative memories:

Now go back and offer each painful item to the Lord for inner healing and leave the burden with Him. Likewise, offer thanksgiving for the good times together. This should give you a balanced perspective on your former marriage. Selectively embrace the good and surrender your rights to nurse your hurts continually.

Divorce often leads to a crisis in faith. Outline and describe your struggle with unbelief in the following areas:

Faith in yourself: ______

Faith in others: ______

Faith in God: ______

Faith in the future: ______

In our despair, we often talk to ourselves in half-truths or untruths to keep our "pity party" going. One way of doing this is to exaggerate or overstate problems beyond realistic limits (I'll *never* be happy again; I'll *always* be a failure; *Everytime* I touch *anything*, it turns to ashes, etc.). Do you use terms like always, never, anything, everything, everyone, etc., to describe your situation? ______ What would be a more realistic way of looking at yourself and your problems? ______

We spend much of our time blaming others for our circumstances. We do not want to "own" our behavior and be responsible for our lives. What circumstances are you blaming on others? ______

What part did you play in shaping these circumstances? ______

When we are hurt it is easy to fall into paralyzing self-pity. List all the reasons you should pity yourself:

Now—read the list to yourself! What has changed in your life as a result of feeling sorry for yourself?

What would be some better ways to deal with self-pity?

Make a list of all the blessings in your life. Spend some time meditating on these and thank the Lord for them

What can you change in your life right now?

What cannot be changed in your life right now?

Knowing what can/cannot be changed, what are you going to do about . . .

What can be changed?

What cannot be changed?

Anxiety about the future takes much of the joy out of our lives. List the anxieties that are plaguing you:

Now, list the anxieties that can be eliminated by further effort or thought:

Of the remaining anxieties, which ones will be resolved through further worry?

Life is often seen as a partnership between God and man in the push and shove of daily life. List ways you think *God* is in control of the daily affairs of your life:

List areas in which you think *you* are responsible:

Do you believe God has your best interest at heart, and is actually working things out "for good for those who love Him"? Explain what has brought you to this conclusion.

Commit yourself to *living*! Memorize and claim the following faith promises for your life (use small note cards to write the scriptures on for easy everyday referral and memorization):

Write out and summarize 1 John 1:9 ______

Summary: ______

Proverbs 3:5-6 ______

Summary: ______

Read and summarize Psalm 103: ______

Summary: ______

Counselor's Comments:

SECTION IV

What Are You Doing?

"*But be doers of the word, and not hearers only, deceiving yourselves. For if anyone is a hearer of the word and not a doer, he is like a man who observes his natural face in a mirror; for he observes himself and goes away and at once forgets what he was like.*" James 1:22-24 (RSV)

It is said that "talk is cheap." You can so easily analyze and diagnose your problems without doing anything about them. You can focus on understanding yourself and keep at arm's length any plans to make your situation better. You can use passivity as a way of resisting change in your life. It is not so much a matter of "can't," but "won't." "I will not change!" To take steps toward tomorrow means laying aside "mourning clothes" and getting on with living again.

God calls you not only to *know* His Word, but to seek to *apply* it to everyday living. You can simply parrot back correct answers without ever testing out those answers in the laboratory of life. But you are called to put feet to your faith, to flesh out in action what you know in theory. This can be a great adventure in faith if you are willing to give it a try. May God give you His grace to take charge of your situation, stepping out in faith to make a better tomorrow.

What Are You Doing?

Part 1 — *Care for Yourself*

What are the major concerns of your life right now? ______

What are you doing to deal with these concerns? ______

What kind of social activities are you involved in? ______

How does your participation/lack of participation meet your needs? ______

What kind of problems do you face as a divorced person in social relationships? ______

What are you doing to deal with these problems? ______

Are you involved in self-improvement programs (i.e., college, vo-tech school, Weight Watchers, Alcoholics Anonymous, etc.? ______

If so, what? ______

If not, why not? ______

What kind of work are you doing? ______

What effect is your divorce having upon your job performance and job potential? Explain: ______

In what ways are you a different person today?

From when you were first married until your divorce: ______

From when you were first divorced to the present: ______

In what ways do you view yourself as a victim of your circumstances? ______

How does such a view of yourself affect the way you act and feel? ______

If today is the first day of the rest of your life, what can you do with your *present* to make your *future* bright? ______

What are you doing to forsake your identity as a married person and establish your identity as a single person?

What kind of identity do co-workers, friends, and relatives want you to assume? (the "swinger," the "mourning widow/widower," the "PTA Parent of the Year," etc.) Describe:

What are your feelings about others trying to shape your identity for you?

What do the significant people of your life desire you to be?

How have you responded to their desires and what has been the result?

What do you find that is positive about being a single person? List five things.

1.

2.

3.

4.

5.

What do you find that is negative about being a single person? List five things.

1.

2.

3.

4. ____

____

5. ____

____

Describe what is the hardest thing to adjust to in single living? ____

____

____

What are you doing to deal with this problem? ____

____

____

____

____

Counselor's Comments:

Part 2 — *Care for Your Spirit*

What do you see as the major obstruction for emotional/spiritual growth in your life?

What are you doing about it?

What changes have you noticed in your spirit as a result of your divorce?

The Bible generally takes a view in opposition to divorce. Examine the following passages and briefly outline what they say about the subject.

Matthew 5:32 & 19:9

Mark 10:1-12

Romans 7:2-3

1 Corinthians 7:10-16

Do you feel your divorce was justified on biblical grounds? ______ If so, please explain:

Since divorce and remarriage do not fit into God's ideal plan for men and women, how are you dealing with this issue spiritually? ______

What do you think God's feelings are toward you in the aftermath of your divorce (wrathful, judgmental and unforgiving, OR loving, understanding and forgiving)? State your *feelings* and give *reasons* why you feel the way you do.

If divorce involves failure and sin against one another, what do the following passages have to say about God's plan for forgiveness and reconciliation?

John 3:16-21 (especially vss. 16-17) ______

1 John 1:5-10 (especially vs. 9) ______

Would you be willing to "believe" (trust in, rely upon) that Christ's death paid your sin debt; would you "confess" (own up to, acknowledge) your sinful acts and attitudes; and would you "repent" (be sorry enough to stop destructive, selfish behavior) which led to your part in the divorce? ______

If so, list acts and attitudes that require you to confess and repent. ______

On a scale of 1 to 10 (1—"turned off," 1—"enthusiastaic"), appraise your interest in spiritual things: ______

In what ways is this demonstrated in your life? ______

What is your present involvement in the church? List what you are doing and what is being done for you. ______

How well is your church serving you?

What needs are being met there? ______

What needs are not being met there? ______

What do you believe God is saying to you in this season of your life? ______

What are you saying to Him? ______

Counselor's Comments:

Part 3 — *Care of Your Finances*

Financial responsiblity plays a crucial part in recovering from divorce. Work out your budget carefully to plan for your future properly.

BUDGET*

Gross Income $ ______________

Fixed Expenses:

Income and payroll taxes $ ______________

Social Security ______________

Union Dues ______________

Tithe (10% of Gross) ______________

Other ______________________________ ______________

______________________________ ______________

Total Fixed Expenses $ ______________ $ ______________

Working Income (Deduct Total Fixed from Gross Income) $ ______________

Budget %

$ ______________ Savings

(10% of Working Income) $ ______________

$ ______________ Living Expenses

(75% of Working Income) $ ______________

	Monthly	Per Pay Period
Mortgage or Rent	$ ______________	$ ______________
Heat	______________	______________
Electricity	______________	______________
Water/Sewage/Garbage	______________	______________
Telephone	______________	______________
Car Insurance	______________	______________
Gasoline	______________	______________
Car Repairs	______________	______________
Recreation/Entertainment	______________	______________
Newspapers/Periodicals	______________	______________
Health Insurance	______________	______________
Car Insurance	______________	______________
Life Insurance	______________	______________
Doctor, Dentist, Medications	______________	______________
Food/Household	______________	______________
Cleaning/Dry Cleaning	______________	______________
Clothes	______________	______________
Home Furnishings	______________	______________
Emergency	______________	______________
Christmas and Gifts	______________	______________
Vacation	______________	______________
Allowances	______________	______________
Other ______________________________	______________	______________
______________________________	______________	______________
TOTAL LIVING EXPENSE	______________	______________

$ ______________ Debts and Buffer (15% of Working Income) $ ______________ $ ______________

______________________________ ______________

______________________________ ______________

______________________________ ______________

______________________________ ______________

______________________________ ______________

______________________________ ______________

TOTAL DEBTS $ ______________ $ ______________

---

*Reprinted by permission from *Your Money Matters* by Malcolm MacGregor, copyright 1977, published by Bethany House Publishers, Minneapolis, Minnesota 55438.

From your budget sheet, list in order the top five major expenditures.

1. ______________________________
2. ______________________________
3. ______________________________
4. ______________________________
5. ______________________________

How do these expenditures fit with the main priorities of your life? (Are you paying for what you want to get out of life?) Explain. ______________________________

____

____

____

____

In what ways have financial problems been the basis for further conflict with your former spouse? ______________

____

____

____

____

____

Counselor's Comments:

Part 4 – *Care for Your Children*

Do you try to be a "super-parent" to your children? ______________ If so, in what ways? ______________

Why? ______________

In what ways, that you are conscious of, are you using your children to hurt your former spouse? ("bad-mouthing" former spouse, making your children "spies" on ex-spouse's social life, cutting off financial support/visitation rights)

What is usually accomplished by such acts? ______________

How do you feel your spouse/your children feel about being used in this way? ______________

Do you ever feel imprisoned by your children (restricted because of them)? If so, how do you deal with this problem?

Do you sense any attempt on the part of one or more of your children to try to fill the role of your ex-spouse? ______________ If so, what are you doing to help them be themselves and forsake the role of substitute spouse/parent? ______________

What feelings have you shared with your children about your divorce? ______________

What has been their reaction to your feelings? ______________

What feelings have your children shared with you regarding the effect of your divorce on their lives? ______________

____

____

____

____

____

____

In what ways have you responded to your children's feelings? ______________

____

____

____

____

What do you do to keep the good memories of your marriage alive for your children? ______________

____

____

____

List five positive memories that you could discuss with your children:

1. ____
2. ____
3. ____
4. ____
5. ____

Counselor's Comments:

SECTION V

Where Are You Going?

> "*Trust in the Lord with all your heart, and do not rely on your own insight. In all your ways acknowledge Him, and He will make straight your paths.*" Proverbs 3:5-6 (RSV)

Embarking in a new direction can bring mixed feelings to your spirit—feelings of eagerness as well as fear. Adventure and security are opposites; you either take some risks and feel insecure or you play it safe and are bored.

This section is a call to adventure! An adventure that will embrace life with all of its hopes and fears, and dare you to go on. It will involve mapping strategies for new patterns of living. It will involve dealing with deadly passivity which would root you permanently in the pain of the past. It will force you to be accountable to the Lord and to yourself for the kind of future you design for your life.

I invite you to do some daring dreaming! Commit your future to the Lord. Begin setting realistic goals that fit your capabilities and God's call on your life. Then venture out courageously, taking concrete steps to make your dreams reality. Trust in the Lord in this process, be sensitive to His leading and correction. Above all, trust in Him to help you make a new beginning of your life.

Where Are You Going?

New beginnings start with the courage to dream! Describe what you would like to accomplish by way of personal growth in the next five years.

Vocationally: ____________________

Financially: ____________________

Socially: ____________________

Emotionally: ____________________

Spiritually: ____________________

What do you propose to do to make your dreams come true in the following areas?

Vocational: ____

Financial: ____

Social: ____

Emotional: ____

Spiritual: ____

Recognize that any reconstruction of your life must begin with foundational issues. Consider your specific plans for *spiritual* reconstruction in the next five years. What will you do to rebuild the following aspects of your spiritual life?

Life of worship (private/public devotional life): ________________________

Life of witness (strategy for sharing your faith): ________________________

Life of service (strategy for using gifts and graces to serve others): ________________

What specific steps are you willing to take to rebuild your emotional life? Describe positive ways in which you can express your feelings to others (admit hurt, express anger, share honestly): ______

In what ways can you change your thinking toward yourself? (inferiority, guilt, self-hatred, imperfection) ______

In what ways are you going to deal with depression? (change of friends, life-style, location, education, vocation) ______

What strategy do you have to reconstruct your social life? Describe positive ways in which you can:

Meet new people/make new friends: ______

Maintain present relationships: ______

Terminate old, painful relationships: ______

Describe your dreams for your children: ______

What will you do during the next five years to make your dreams for your children come true? ______

______

______

______

______

The separation of divorce is often characterized by unloving behavior and abusive treatment of ourselves and others. In what ways are you willing to love again?

Love yourself: ______

______

______

______

______

______

Love others: ______

______

______

______

______

______

Counselor's Comments:

Contract for New Beginnings

I will deal with my past:

By forsaking the following destructive attitudes and actions toward myself:

By forsaking destructive attitudes and actions toward others:

By forsaking destructive attitudes and actions toward God:

I will deal with my present:

By seeking to love myself in the following ways:

By seeking to love others in the following ways:

By seeking to love God in the following ways:

I will deal with my future:

By setting the following goals which will help me grow personally:

By setting the following goals which will help me grow socially:

By setting the following goals which will help me grow spiritually:

APPENDIX 1
Group Leader's Guide

This section is designed to be used by a group leader to stimulate and direct positive discussion. The leader should be assisted by one other person who can help clarify issues for the leader and the participants. It is further suggested that it be a "closed group," that is, allowing no new members into the group once the process is started. This will assist in creating a confidential environment, conducive to sharing at a deeper level than otherwise possible in an "open group." The program could be modular, running quarterly or semi-annually (as people express interest), with an on-going care/support group being made available once the structured group-counseling process is completed.

Time should not be an intimidating factor; encourage counselees to work ahead only enough to cover the material you plan to discuss. Some sections will need more attention than others, depending on the needs of the group. Leaders should be sensitive to this issue and pace the process accordingly. Ideally the program should be covered in 1½-2 hours per week over a period of six to eight weeks. It can also be structured into a two-day weekend retreat, with individuals completing the worksheets prior to the sessions.

The questions are designed to avoid yes/no or short answers, so as to elicit the greatest possible response. The questions listed are merely suggestive, and space is provided for additional questions that may be added by the leader. Costs for the program may be underwritten by the church, or the leader may wish to charge each individual a fee for materials, thus committing participants to the program through their investment.

SECTION I—**Who Are You?**

1. Describe your childhood (ages 1-18). What significant events influenced your life positively and negatively during this time?
2. Describe your parents. What were they like? In what ways did they influence your life positively and negatively?
3. Describe the ways your parents related to each other. In what ways did they show their love and express their anger toward one another?
4. Describe yourself in terms of positive and negative traits. In what ways do you think you will be remembered when you are gone?
5. Describe your past values. What has been important to you?
6. Describe your past goals. Which ones have been achieved/not achieved?
7. Describe the most significant experience in your life.
8. Who has had the greatest impact on your life? Describe in what ways that person has affected you.
9. Describe your past social life. What kinds of influence (positive/negative) have your friends made on your life?
10. Describe your spiritual life to date. What has happened in your relationship to God and how has that affected you and those around you?

Counselor's Additional Questions:

___

___

___

___

___

___

___

___

___

___

___

SECTION II—**Where Have You Been?**

1. Describe your courtship with your former spouse. What attracted you to him/her? What interests did you share? What made you finally decide to get married?
2. Describe your former spouse in terms of positive/negative character traits.
3. Describe your expectations regarding your marriage before going to the altar. What do you think were your spouse's expectations?
4. Describe your first year of marriage. What were your successes and what were your disappointments?
5. What goals and values did you share/not share?
6. When and in what ways did you sense trouble in your marriage? What did you do, or not do, to rescue the relationship?
7. Describe ways that you believe you contributed to the breakdown of your relationship. In what ways do you feel your former spouse contributed to the breakup?
8. What were your feelings about getting a divorce?
9. Describe how your divorce affected your life in terms of relationships with relatives, friends and children.
10. Describe how your divorce has affected you in the following ways (address one at a time): emotionally, socially, economically and spiritually.
11. Describe personal traits that you feel make you lovable and worth knowing as a person.

Counselor's Additional Questions:

SECTION III—**What Are You Thinking and Feeling?**

1. In what ways are you dealing with your anger and guilt resulting from your divorce?
2. Describe your present feelings about your divorce. Where do you place yourself in the grieving process?
3. Describe your feelings about asking for and offering forgiveness for past actions.
4. Describe how you have handled the judgment of others as a result of your divorce.
5. What lessons did you learn from your divorce (particularly, what did you learn about yourself)?
6. What are some of the positive memories of your past relationship?
7. What are you doing to "unpack" mentally from your journey through divorce and to "get on with your life"?
8. What *can* be changed that needs to be changed in your life? What *cannot* be changed right now?
9. Describe the anxieties present in your life right now. In what ways can these be eliminated by personal effort?
10. Describe ways in which you believe God is working things out for good in your life.

Counselor's Additional Questions:

SECTION IV—**What Are You Doing?**

1. Describe your social life, positively and negatively.
2. What are you doing to rehabilitate yourself (self-improvement programs, schooling, travel)? What is this doing to make you feel good about yourself?
3. Describe how your divorce has affected your employment (job performance/potential). How have you dealt with the conflict between family responsibilities and the demands of your work?
4. In what ways are you a different person since your divorce? How does this perception affect the way you feel and act?
5. What are you doing in the *present* to make your *future* bright?
6. Describe your positive and negative feelings about being a single person.
7. Describe what you see as the biggest obstruction for emotional/spiritual growth in your life. What are you doing about it?
8. Describe how you have dealt with the link in the Bible between divorce and moral failure. What kind of difficulties have you encountered in attempting to confess and repent of spiritually destructive attitudes and actions?
9. Describe your relationship with your children. In what ways has your divorce affected your relationship with your children?
10. Describe the major adjustments you have had to make in becoming a single parent or a separated parent. What have you done to maintain a good relationship with your children?

Counselor's Additional Questions:

SECTION V—**Where Are You Going?**

1. Describe what you would like to accomplish in the following areas in the next five years: vocational, financial, social, emotional and spiritual.
2. Describe steps you are taking in the following areas to make your dreams a reality: vocational, financial, social, emotional and spiritual.
3. Describe how you will reconstruct your spiritual life, in terms of *worship, witness* and *service.*
4. Describe ways you can change your *thinking* and *feeling* about yourself and others.
5. Describe ways you can reconstruct your social life, in terms of *terminating* some relationships, maintaining present relationships and *starting* new relationships.
6. Describe your dreams for your children. What are you doing to make these dreams reality?
7. Describe ways in which you will love yourself, love others and love God.
8. Describe what you are going to do to forsake destructive past attitudes and actions toward *yourself, others* and *God.*
9. Describe what goals you have selected to help you grow *personally, socially* and *spiritually.*

Counselor's Additional Questions:

APPENDIX 2

Annual Check-up

(To be filled out and returned to counselor one year after counseling sessions)

What have I done to improve my life in the past year?

Emotionally: ____________________

Socially: ____________________

Vocationally: ____________________

Financially:

Spiritually:

What promises, made to myself, have I kept over the past year?

In terms of the past:

In terms of the present:

In terms of the future:

What goals have I achieved in the past year?

What goals have not been achieved in the past year? List and describe what prevented them from being achieved:

Establish new goals for the next year. Be realistic.

Personal goals:

Relational goals:

Spiritual goals:

APPENDIX 3

Ten Commandments for Formerly Marrieds*

1. Thou shalt not live in thy past.
2. Thou shalt be responsible for thy present and not blame thy past for it.
3. Thou shalt not feel sorry for thyself indefinitely.
4. Thou shalt assume thy end of the blame for thy marriage dissolvement.
5. Thou shalt not try to reconcile thy past and reconstruct thy future by a quick, new marriage.
6. Thou shalt not make thy children the victims of thy past marriage.
7. Thou shalt not spend all thy time trying to convince thy children how terrible and evil their departed parent is.
8. Thou shalt learn all thou canst about being a one-parent family and get on with it.
9. Thou shalt ask others for help when thou needest it.
10. Thou shalt ask God for the wisdom to bury yesterday, create today and plan tomorrow.

*Jim Smoke, *Growing Through Divorce*, copyright, 1976, Harvest House Publishers, 1075 Arrowsmith, Eugene, Oregon 97402.

APPENDIX 4

Resources

Books on Divorce

Duty, Guy. *Divorce and Remarriage.* Minneapolis: Bethany House Publishers, 1967.
Laney, J. Carl. *The Divorce Myth.* Minneapolis: Bethany House Publishers, 1981.
Murray, John. *Divorce.* Philadelphia: Orthodox Presbyterian Church, 1953.
Small, Dwight H. *The Right to Remarry.* Old Tappan, NJ: Fleming H. Revell Company, 1975.
Smoke, Jim. *Growing Through Divorce.* Eugene, OR: Harvest House Publishers, 1976.

Books on Emotional Growth

Backus, William & Chapian, Marie. *Telling Yourself the Truth.* Minneapolis: Bethany House Publishers, 1980.
Berne, Eric. *Games People Play.* New York: Grove Press, Inc., 1964.
Frankl, Viktor E. *Man's Search for Meaning.* New York: Pocket Books, 1959.
Guinness, Os. *In Two Minds—The Dilemma of Doubt and How To Resolve It.* Downers Grove, IL: InterVarsity Press, 1976.
James, Muriel and Jongeward, Dorothy. *Born To Win.* Philippines: Addison-Wesley Publishing Company, 1971.
Jones, Martyn-Lloyd. *Spiritual Depression.* Grand Rapids, Michigan: William B. Eerdmans Publishing Company, 1965.
O'Connor, Elizabeth. *Our Many Selves.* New York: Harper & Row, Publishers, 1971.
Osborne, Cecil. *The Art of Understanding Yourself.* Grand Rapids, MI: Zondervan Publishing House, 1968.
Powell, John. *Fully Human, Fully Alive.* Niles, IL: Argus Communications, 1976.
________. *Why Am I Afraid To Love?* Niles, IL: Argus Communications, 1972.
________. *Why Am I Afraid To Tell You Who I Am?* Niles, IL: Argus Communications, 1969.
Tournier, Paul. *Guilt and Grace.* New York: Harper & Row, Publishers, 1962.
________. *The Meaning of Persons.* New York: Harper & Row, Publishers, 1957.
________. *A Place for You.* New York: Harper & Row, Publishers, 1968.
________. *The Person Reborn.* New York: Harper & Row, Publishers, 1966.
________. *The Strong and the Weak.* Philadelphia: The Westminster Press, 1963.
White, John. *Eros Defiled—The Christian and Sexual Sin.* Downers Grove, IL: InterVarsity Press, 1977.
Wright, H. Norman. *The Christian Use of Emotional Power.* Old Tappan, NJ: Fleming H. Revell Company, 1974.

Books on Spiritual Development

Christenson, Larry. *Back to Square One.* Minneapolis; Bethany House Publishers, 1979.
________. *The Renewed Mind.* Minneapolis: Bethany House Publishers, 1974.
Elliot, Elisabeth. *A Slow and Certain Light.* Waco, TX: Word Books, 1973.
Hegre, T. A. *The Cross and Sanctification.* Minneapolis: Bethany House Publishers, 1960.
Lewis, C. S. *Mere Christianity.* New York: The Macmillan Company, 1943.
________. *The Problem of Pain.* New York: The Macmillan Company, 1962.
Marshall, Catherine. *Something More.* New York: McGraw-Hill, 1974.
Murray, Andrew. *The Believer's School of Prayer.* Minneapolis: Bethany House Publishers, 1982.
Nee, Watchman. *The Normal Christian Life.* Fort Washington, PA: Christian Literature Crusade, 1963.
Packer, J. I. *Knowing God.* Downers Grove, IL: InterVarsity Press, 1973.
Schaeffer, Edith. *Affliction.* Old Tappan, NJ: Fleming H. Revell Company, 1978.
Schaeffer, Francis A. *The God Who Is There.* Chicago: InterVarsity Press, 1968.
Sproul, R. C. *If There Is a God, Why Are There Atheists?* Minneapolis: Bethany House Publishers, 1978.
Stott, John R. W. *Basic Christianity.* Downers Grove, IL: InterVarsity Press, 1971.
Taylor, Richard Shelley. *The Disciplined Life.* Minneapolis: Bethany House Publishers, 1962.
Thielicke, Helmut. *Life Can Begin Again.* Philadelphia: The Fortress Press, 1963.
Tozer, A. W. *The Pursuit of God.* Harrisburg. PA: Christian Publications, 1948.